W9-BMM-499

HEY,
Sports
Fans!

HEY,
Sports
Fans!

OVER 150 SILLY SPORTS
JOKES AND RIDDLES

by **MICHAEL MORGAN PELLOWSKI**

illustrated by
MATT PELLOWSKI

A TRUMPET CLUB ORIGINAL BOOK

No part of this publication may be reproduced in whole or in part, or stored in a retrieval system, or transmitted in any form or by any means, electronic, mechanical, photocopying, recording, or otherwise, without written permission of the publisher. For information regarding permission, write to Scholastic Inc., 555 Broadway, New York, NY 10012.

ISBN 0-590-98102-1

Copyright © 1996 by Scholastic Inc. All rights reserved. Published by Scholastic Inc. TRUMPET and the TRUMPET logo are registered trademarks of Scholastic Inc.

12 11 10 9 8 7 6 5 4 3 2   6 7 8 9/9 0 1/0

Printed in the U.S.A.

To the best team a father ever played with . . .
Judy, Morgan, Matt, Melanie and Martin

CONTENTS

PUNCHLINES

How do you keep a herd of steer in shape?
Make them do cow-isthenics.

BODY BUILDER: I'm as strong as a horse.
TRAINER: Whoa boy! Don't exaggerate.

LITTLE GIRL: Are you a good soccer player?
LITTLE BOY: Yes. I'm so good I can play the game with no hands.

1

FARMER: Your baseball landed in my chicken coop.
LITTLE BOY: Now that's definitely fowl territory.

BOY: I run every morning.
GIRL: You mean you jog before class?
BOY: No. I get up late and have to chase the school bus!

FRED: I can jump rope fifty times without missing.
ED: What?
FRED: I can jump rope fifty times without missing.
ED: What?
FRED: Oh skip it!

What do you do to a naughty boxer?
Make him sit in a corner.

What is a boxer's favorite drink?
Fruit punch.

MATT: I know an athlete who's happy every time he strikes out.

PAT: He must be a terrible baseball player.

MATT: Yeah, but he's a good bowler.

CUSTOMER: Do you have any dumbbells in this sporting goods store?

CLERK: No sir. All of our salespeople are very smart.

MOE: Why are you playing fullback?
BEAU: I took a quarterback test and couldn't pass.

What did Mr. Scrooge wear to play hockey?
Cheap skates.

What is the most popular position on a football team?
The center of attention.

COACH: What do you drink before a marathon?
ATHLETE: Lots of running water.

COACH: What did the gymnast do when you fired him?
MANAGER: He flipped!

OUTFIELDER: What's round and covered with dirt?
INFIELDER: A ground ball.

Which of Santa's reindeer is a track star?
100-yard Dasher.

How can you tell if an elephant is a prize-fighter?
He'll be wearing boxing trunks!

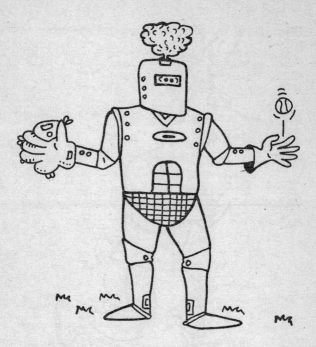

COACH: Why did you come to the baseball stadium dressed in a suit of armor?
ATHLETE: You told me this was a knight game.

What do joggers wash with?
Running water.

Why did the boxer wear ballet shoes?
His manager told him to dance around the ring.

MEL: I'm really tired. I just played basketball against a kangaroo.
NEL: I'm more tired. I just played soccer against a goat.
DEL: Ha! I'm the most tired. I just arm wrestled with an octopus!

MRS. THUMB: Tom Thumb, where are you going?
TOM: I'm going out to play miniature golf, Mom.

Why was the racehorse upset?
He was saddled with a lot of problems.

ED: Do kangaroos make good basketball players?

FRED: Yes. They have great jump shots.

MIKE: Are umpires good eaters?

SPIKE: Yes. They always clean their plates.

AL: Do joggers catch colds?

HAL: No, but they get runny noses.

RON: Why doesn't Big Foot play baseball?

DON: He's a big track star.

BASEBALL DIAMOND SPARKLERS

Which baseball team also takes care of sick animals?
The New York Vets.

What plant set a record for hitting home-runs?
Babe Root.

What has a pig on third base, a cow in the outfield, and a goat on pitcher's mound?
A baseball farm team.

Why is an umpire like a salesman?
Because they both make a lot of unpopular calls.

What yellow vegetable was a famous ball player?
Ty Corn Cobb.

Which superhero do baseball players like the best?
Batman.

Which baseball player never travels with the team?
The left-behind fielder.

Which baseball league has teams of talking birds?

The myna league.

What dog do you find at a baseball stadium?

The catcher's mutt.

How is a baseball glove like a spider?
They both use webbing to catch things.

How did the baseball player burn his fingers?
He caught a sizzling line drive.

What does a catcher wear on a cold day?
Catcher's mittens.

What's round and buzzes around a garbage can?
A fly ball.

Why did the baseball players go to the park?
To enjoy the swings.

Why was the baseball player's mother happy?
Her son reached home safely.

Why was the crow mad?
He got cawed out on strikes.

Why did the ghost go to the baseball game?
To boo the umpire.

SPOIL SPORTS

What do you get if you cross a baseball player with a race horse?
Someone who's good at pitching horseshoes.

Sports Flash!
Grimy billiard experts always play dirty pool.

What do you get if you cross a baseball pitcher and a boxer?

A player who throws a lot of fights.

What do you get if you cross a rabbit with a tennis court?

A hare net.

Sports Flash!

Pro tennis players earn net profits.

What do you get if you cross a boxer and a bowler?

A punch bowl.

What do you get if you cross a burglar with a baseball player?

A guy who steals bases.

What do you get if you cross a body-builder with a defensive back?

A very strong safety.

What do you get if you cross a telephone operator with a marathon?

A long-distance runner.

Sports Flash!

Softball pitchers are underhanded people.

What do you call . . .

a long-distance runner who always grins?

A miler smiler.

What do you call . . .

a father who carries his son's golf clubs?
A daddy caddy.

an angel who stops the puck from going in the net?
A holy goalie.

a baseball slugger with a sour disposition?
A bitter hitter.

a chubby person who rides a horse in a race?
A stocky jockey.

a narrow room where weight lifters work out?
A slim gym.

an amphibian who runs for exercise?
A frogger jogger.

someone who makes a pest of himself at Wimbledon?
A tennis menace.

HOOP HA-HA'S

Why did the basketball player bring her car to practice?
She wanted to drive to the basket.

What rabbit plays pro basketball?
Hare Jordan.

Why are basketball courts slippery?
Players dribble on them.

Where would you find a goose on a basketball court?

At the water fowl line.

How did the baby basketball player's shirt get wet?

He dribbled on himself.

Why did the teller make the basketball team?

He had a great bank shot.

What kind of basketball nets do they use in Hawaii?
Hula hoops.

Why did the basketball player take up fishing?
He wanted to master a hook shot.

Why do basketball players always stay home?
Because they aren't supposed to travel.

SPORTS SNICKERS

What did the newspaper editor yell to the bodybuilder?
Stop the presses!

What's furry and cheers at a game?
A root bear.

What rock singer from England is a famous runner?
Mick Jogger.

What do you call an angry competitor in a marathon?
A very cross-country runner.

What is a hog's favorite sport?
Pig pong.

Do skunks ever study karate?
No. They're masters of kung phew!

What do you call an aerobic acorn?
A fitness nut.

What do young cows get when they lift weights?
Great calf muscles.

Which insect do you find in a bowling alley?
A bowl weevil.

What kind of team has no player over 18 on it?
A minor league baseball team.

What did the prizefighter give his fiancée?
A boxing ring.

How do you pry an umpire away from home plate?
Use umplyers.

Who rules the bowling alley?
The King Pin.

What's the first rule of boxing?
Never get caught lying down on the job.

Which baseball team has ghost players?
The Toronto Boojays.

What did Santa Claus do at the football game?
He gave a little Christmas cheer.

Why did the coach put Gretel in the soccer game but not Hans?
Using Hans is illegal in soccer.

Why couldn't the caterpillar go out for the swim team?
He wasn't old enough to do the butterfly stroke.

What's the sharpest dive a swimmer can do?
A jackknife.

What purrs and loves bowling?
An alley cat.

Why did the jogger get in trouble?
He ran away from home.

In what sport do athletes ride sea horses?
Water polo.

Why did the wrestler bring a key to the match?
To get out of a headlock.

Why did the absent-minded professor take up running?
She wanted to jog her memory.

Why did Dracula join the baseball team?
He wanted to be the bat boy.

Which football player tells the best stories?
The taleback.

What sport do bus drivers love?
Greyhound races.

When is the worst time to call a baseball player?
When he's out.

Which hockey team is Smokey the Bear's favorite?
The New York Forest Rangers.

How can you tell if a boxer took a bath?
There will be a ring around the tub.

Why did the baseball player wear swimming trunks to the stadium?
He wanted to practice diving catches.

What does a cool football player wear around his waist?
Very hip pads.

What sport do Mickey and Minnie play?
Mice hockey.

Why did the baseball umpire take judo lessons?
So she could throw players out of the game.

What did the quarterback say to the flower bulbs?
Root for the team, guys.

FOOTBALL FUNNIES

Who delivers mail to football players?
The goal postman.

What do you call a blizzard in the middle of a football game?
A halftime snow.

What has wings and plays defensive line?
A flying tackle.

What does a quarterback become after eating a big meal?
A fullback.

What position did the zombie play on the football team?
Dead end.

What do you get if you cross a football player and a telephone operator?
A guy with a jersey phone number.

Why did the defensive end wear his uniform to math class?
Because he had some tough math problems to tackle.

How do you stop an opposing team's fly patterns?
Use a screen play.

Why is a quarterback like a scoutmaster?
They both call a lot of hikes.

How can a football player remain anonymous?

Wear an unlisted number.

Why do quarterbacks do well in school?

They know how to pass their courses.

Which football team is named after tiny bottles of pop?
The Mini-soda Vikings.

Why don't football players get hot?
Because there are always fans around.

What is the cleanest play in football?
The sweep.

Which deer is a great quarterback?
Doe Montana.

What pass patterns do the Miami Dolphins hate?
Hook patterns.

Why did the halfback wear swimming trunks?
His coach told him to run dive plays.

Why did the coach put a magician in the backfield?

He wanted to run a trick play.

Why did the quarterback put his eggs in a mixer?

Because he loved to scramble.

What has feathers and weighs 300 pounds?

A down lineman.

What do you get when offensive linemen stand on one foot?

An unbalanced line.

How do offensive linemen celebrate after a game?

They have a block party.

GOLF GIGGLES & TENNIS TICKLERS

HO-HO-HO!

18

PLOP

Why was Santa Claus happy?
He made a ho-ho-hole in one.

What do golfers do on rainy days?
They putter around the house.

What do golf socks look like?
They're green and have 18 holes in them.

Why is a bad golfer like a motorboat?
They both go putt-putt-putt.

What do you call a tennis player who plays tricks?
A court jester.

What did one tennis racket say to the other?
Get a grip on yourself, pal.

Why don't golfers have wrinkled clothes?
They carry irons in their bags.

When do English golfers meet on the course?
At tee time.

What is the hottest part of a tennis game?
The end of a match.

Where do kings and queens play tennis?
At their royal courts.

Why did the tennis fan go to an eye doctor?
Because every time he watched a match, he saw doubles.

Why don't romantic tennis players care if they're poor?
Because in tennis when you have nothing, it's really love.

What does a tennis player do when he's in love?
He goes courting.

Which bird is a famous tennis player?
John McEncrow.

What do you call a golfer who thinks about shooting under par?
A birdie brain.

What do golfers eat for lunch?
Club sandwiches.

Why is a tennis player like a judge?
Because you find both of them in a court.

KNOCKOUTS

Knock, knock!
Who's there?
Dizzy.
Dizzy who?
Dizzy know how to dribble a basketball?

Knock, knock!
Who's there?
Venice.
Venice who?
Venice the last game of the season?

Knock, knock!
Who's there?
Ron.
Ron who?
Ron fast if you want to win the race.

Knock, knock!
Who's there?
Canoe.
Canoe who?
Canoe dunk a basketball?

Knock, knock!
Who's there?
Formosa.
Formosa who?
Formosa the game I sat on the bench.

Knock, knock!
Who's there?
Avenue.
Avenue who?
Avenue scored a touchdown this year?

Knock, knock!
Who's there?
Butternut.
Butternut who?
Butternut argue with the umpire.

Knock, knock!
Who's there?
Tamara.
Tamara who?
Tamara we play a home game.

Knock, knock!
Who's there?
A herd.
A herd who?
A herd this pitcher throws fastballs.

Knock, knock!
Who's there?
Sherwood.
Sherwood who?
Sherwood like to hit a homerun!

Knock, knock!
Who's there?
Willie.
Willie who?
Willie let me pitch today?

Knock, knock!
Who's there?
Recall.
Recall who?
Recall the plays as we see 'em.

Knock, knock!
Who's there?
Tennis.
Tennis who?
Tennis more than nine.

Knock, knock!
Who's there?
Yule.
Yule who?
Yule be a good player if you practice a lot.

Knock, knock!
Who's there?
Humus.
Humus who?
Humus not argue with the umpire.

Knock, knock!
Who's there?
Toucan.
Toucan who?
Toucan play tennis on the same side if it's a doubles match.

Knock, knock!
Who's there?
Iran.
Iran who?
Iran around the bases, but was thrown out at home.

Knock, knock!
Who's there?
Foreign.
Foreign who?
Foreign the sixth inning and foreign the seventh makes eight runs.

Knock, knock!
Who's there?
Wail.
Wail who?
Wail run two miles tomorrow.